The Legend of Wisconsin

Written by Kathy-jo Wargin
and Illustrated by David Geister

To all those who shared Nanabush stories with me when I was
a young girl growing up in northern Minnesota. Thank you for
inspiring a lifelong love of our beautiful Great Lakes region.

Kathy-jo

—

To all my wonderful family and friends who live throughout
my beautiful, childhood state of Wisconsin, especially
Grandma Ethel, Chris, Danny, Susie, Jimmy, and Beth.

David

—

Illustrator's Acknowledgements

Special thanks are due to Steve Schreader, who was the model for my paintings of Nanabush, even though we never get to see his face, and to my friend, Aaron Novodvorsky, who gave me his usual helpful suggestions. And as always, thanks to my dear wife, Pat Bauer, the muse and critic who supported me with her love and a steady supply of snacks.

Sleeping Bear Press

310 North Main Street, Suite 300
Chelsea, MI 48118
www.sleepingbearpress.com

© 2007 Thomson Gale, a part of the Thomson Corporation.

Thomson, Star Logo and Sleeping Bear Press are trademarks
and Gale is a registered trademark used herein under license.

Printed and bound in Canada.

First Edition

10 9 8 7 6 5 4 3 2 1

Library of Congress Cataloging-in-Publication Data

Wargin, Kathy-jo.
The legend of Wisconsin / written by Kathy-jo Wargin ;
illustrated by David Geister.
p. cm.
Summary: "Gitchee Manitou sends Nanabush the Giant Hare to the new north country to give the first animals their names and special markings. Legend says a game between the Nanabush and Ahmik the Giant Beaver etches out the islands, ponds, and lakes of Wisk-on-sin, which means place of the beaver"
—Provided by publisher.
ISBN 978-1-58536-308-7
1. Legends—Wisconsin. 2. Nanabush (Legendary character)—Legends.
I. Geister, David. II. Title.
GR110.W5W37 2007
398.209775—dc2   22006026004

About the
Legend of Wisconsin

To the Algonquin people of the Great Lakes, Nanabush (also known as Nanabozho, Wenabojo, Manabozho and more) is a trickster hero sent to Earth to name all plants and animals, and to teach the first people how to live a good and prosperous life.

As a young girl growing up in northern Minnesota, I heard many varied Nanabush tales about how our natural features came to be. These beautiful and imaginative stories reflect our heritage, as well as our place in time in the Great Lakes. We have been a culture in transition for generations in this region, and just as we have blended our lives, we have also blended our stories, legends, customs and traditions, and the result is an evolving reflection of who we are as a Great Lakes society.

Specifically, Wisconsin has long been a place where cultures meet, each with their own language and tradition. Because of this, the exact origin of the word Wisconsin is obscure and complex. When Father Jacques Marquette first called the Wisconsin River "Meskousing" in a journal, it was later misread and rewritten as Ouisconsing, and then later as Ouisconsin. Gradually the word was Americanized into "Wisconsin."

As complicated as the evolution of the word itself, many varied thoughts on its definition have existed over the years. Some of those definitions have included a grassy place, a gathering of waters, place of the beaver, muskrat house, and river running through a red place.

From the creation of the Wisconsin River to the Apostle Islands and more, may you explore the many versions of these tales, from the most traditional to the newest. May you enjoy this version too, and be inspired to follow in the footsteps of Nanabush and his friends.

Long ago in a northern land
lived Nanabush the Great Hare.

This was a time when Earth was young and all meadows were yet unbroken. This was a time when deep-colored flowers grew wild along wooded shores, and wetlands were filled with wild fowl and willows. It was a time so new that nothing but trees cast shadows upon the mosses and ferns below. Most of all, this was a time not long after Nanabush had tamed the great freshwater sea, demanding it grow smaller until it parted into five lakes, creating these new lands and places unnamed.

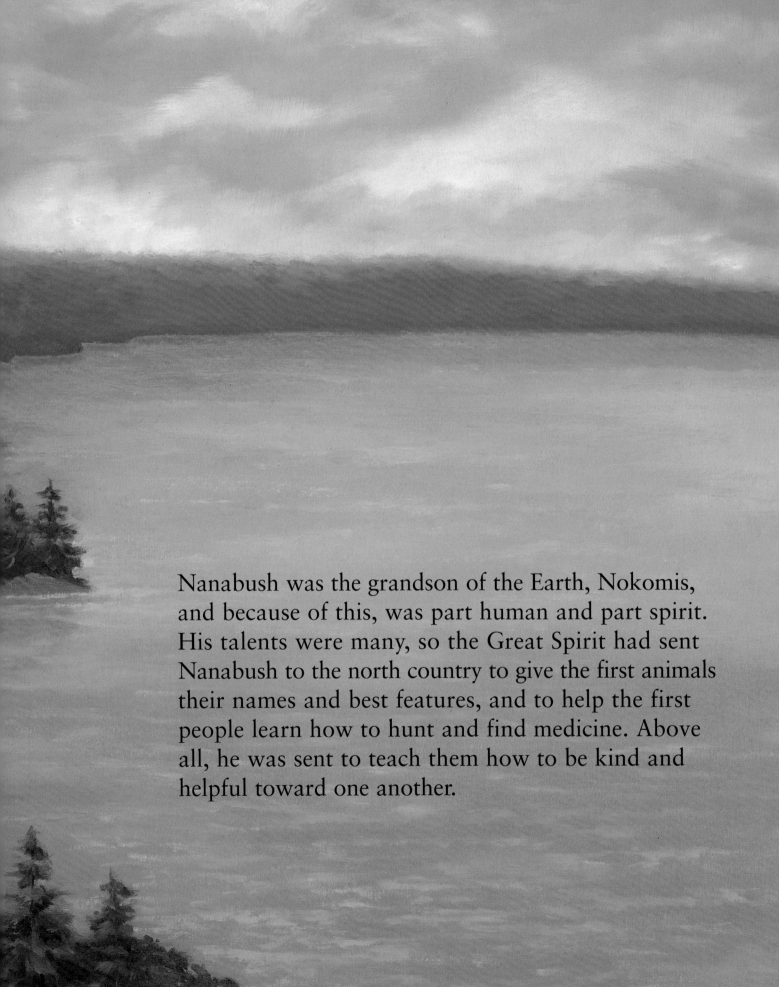

Nanabush was the grandson of the Earth, Nokomis, and because of this, was part human and part spirit. His talents were many, so the Great Spirit had sent Nanabush to the north country to give the first animals their names and best features, and to help the first people learn how to hunt and find medicine. Above all, he was sent to teach them how to be kind and helpful toward one another.

But Nanabush was also a trickster, and could change his shape whenever he wished. Some days he played tricks on the first people and animals. In return, the animals and people played tricks on Nanabush. Although most thought it was amusing to make Nanabush look foolish, none enjoyed it more than Ahmik the Giant Beaver.

One day, Nanabush sat upon the shore of the big northern lake, admiring its beauty and breadth. He was not far from the turning rapids of a great fishing river, and the place where Ahmik often stayed. Little by little, Nanabush noticed the water was rising. He began to worry, for soon it would overtake the land.

Nanabush had no idea what was causing this to happen, so he began to dance around in a worried and foolish manner. As he jumped about, he began to hear a light *chuk! chuk! chuk!* in the distance. Right away he knew it was Ahmik laughing and poking fun at him. When Nanabush discovered that Ahmik had built a dam to trick him into looking foolish, he did not laugh. Instead the Great Hare began to chase Ahmik.

Ahmik slipped into the lake and swam
toward the west. Nanabush stayed close
behind, nearly able to catch him.

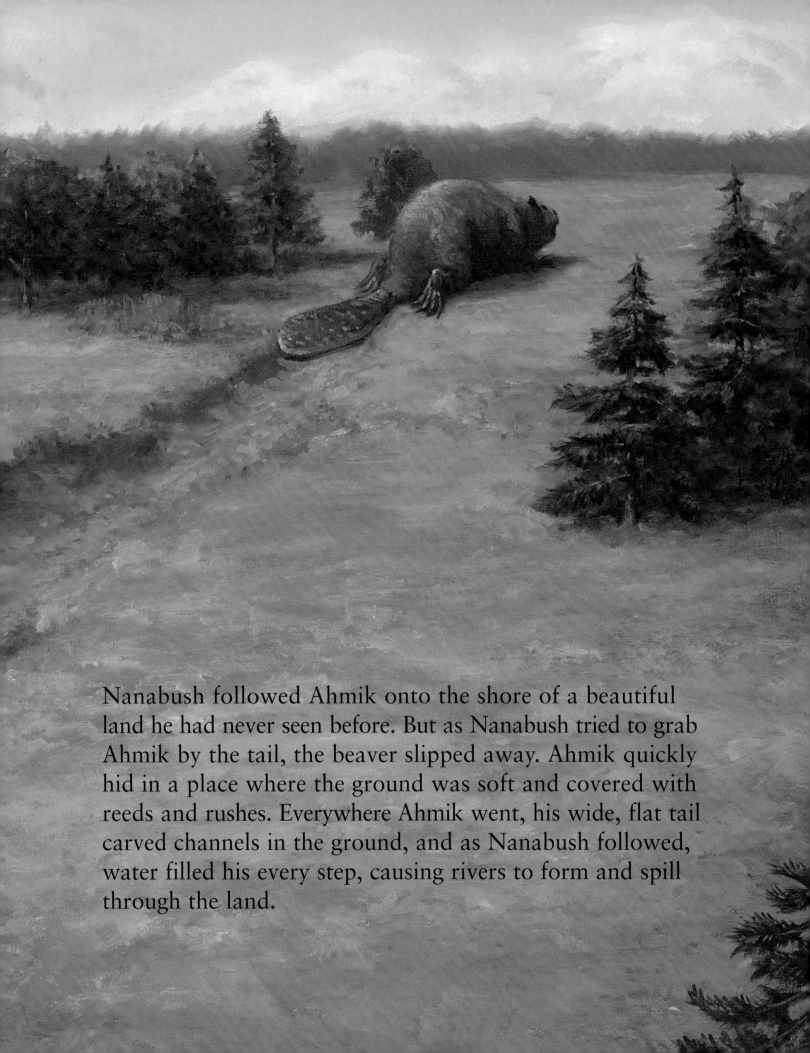

Nanabush followed Ahmik onto the shore of a beautiful land he had never seen before. But as Nanabush tried to grab Ahmik by the tail, the beaver slipped away. Ahmik quickly hid in a place where the ground was soft and covered with reeds and rushes. Everywhere Ahmik went, his wide, flat tail carved channels in the ground, and as Nanabush followed, water filled his every step, causing rivers to form and spill through the land.

Ahmik kept running, but Nanabush was drawing closer. When Nanabush came to the edge of a lake, he spotted a black bear wading in the shallows. The bear spotted Nanabush at the same time, and remembered how the Great Hare had once swatted his nose. The bear grew cross all over again and began to chase Nanabush.

With the bear close behind him, Nanabush quickly grabbed a handful of stones and cast them out into the water. One by one, they grew very large. The stones grew so large they appeared as if they were crawling across the lake. Nanabush quickly skipped across to the other side, leaving the bear behind him. Within moments Nanabush was once again only steps behind Ahmik.

But in an instant, the beaver ran northwest and slipped into a hole in the stony hillside. When Nanabush spotted him there, he called for water to fill the steep ravine where Ahmik was waiting, and the Great Spirit answered his call. Ahmik had no choice but to dig his way out as the water kept falling over the edge of the rocks and filling the gorge. Nanabush was pleased to see this, and so thanked the Great Spirit with a loud voice. The Great Spirit responded with a roaring thunder that rolled through the gorge, filling the air and the falling water with a beautiful echo.

But when Nanabush looked for Ahmik, he
was already off in the distance. Nanabush began
to follow him again when all of a sudden he was stopped
by a loud hissing sound.

And there it was. The most giant serpent of all was facing
Nanabush. The serpent told him that he was searching for the
salted sea. The Great Hare pointed in the direction of a long and
deep river far to his west, and told the snake to follow it south-
ward until it emptied into a great body of salted water. As the
snake went on its way, twisting and turning upon the land, it
carved a long path of rocky cliffs and crags and gorges that soon
filled with water. And as it pushed through tight stony places,
Nanabush heard the sound of rocks striking together in its wake.

Nanabush pursued Ahmik across the land for many months, and was growing tired of the game. But Ahmik the beaver was not growing tired of the chase at all, for he liked finding new ways to make Nanabush look foolish by outwitting him.

Tired and wanting to catch Ahmik more than ever, Nanabush came up with a plan. He knew that Ahmik was resting in a large bay of the big northern lake. As Ahmik splashed about, Nanabush went quietly to the open end of the bay and began to build a dam to trap the beaver. He used the biggest logs and heaviest mud he could find so Ahmik could not escape. Day after day Nanabush worked silently so Ahmik would not notice him. When he was finished, the dam went from shore to shore and Nanabush was certain that he had finally caught Ahmik.

But when Nanabush slipped to the other side of the dam to surprise Ahmik, he wasn't there. The water was calm and waveless, and all that remained was a hole in the bottom of the dam.

Ahmik had escaped. Nanabush was so angry that he began to destroy the dam, tossing the logs and mud and rocks over his shoulder. As he did, the pieces fell and scattered into the water, turning into many islands throughout the lake.

Nanabush was still near the dam when he heard a light chukking sound in the distance. Right away he knew it was Ahmik, laughing at him once more.

At that moment, Nanabush smiled. Even though he did not catch Ahmik, he looked across the land and saw the ponds and lakes his footsteps had made. He saw the kettle-like dips and the gentle swales of soft grassy places where he sat down to rest. He saw a great stone river and all the places where waters gathered amidst the land. He saw thundering waterfalls, wide-turning rivers and beautiful dells. Last, he saw the islands he had made by tossing logs and mud into the water.

Nanabush stood proud above all that was created while chasing Ahmik. The land that came to be was now a place of green and golden meadows settled around shining lakes and rocky hillsides. It was a place of winding rivers and deep forests. It was a place that would someday be known to all as Wisconsin.

Today the footsteps of Nanabush and Ahmik remind us how the beautiful land of Wisconsin came to be. And although Nanabush did not win the first chase, he and Ahmik are with us still, lingering upon the shores and in the deepest forests, each one waiting patiently, ready to go on with the chase.

Kathy-jo Wargin

Author Kathy-jo Wargin has earned national acclaim with numerous best-selling children's titles such as *B is for Badger: A Wisconsin Alphabet* and *The Edmund Fitzgerald: Song of the Bell*. Born in Tower, Minnesota and inspired by the cultural stories she heard as a child, Kathy-jo has dedicated her career to exploring the folklore of the Upper Midwest.

In addition to *The Legend of Wisconsin*, she is also the author of several titles in Sleeping Bear's award-winning Legends series, which includes *The Legend of Old Abe*; *The Legend of Minnesota*; *The Legend of the Lady's Slipper*, an Upper Midwest Bookseller's Favorite; and *The Legend of the Loon*, an IRA Children's Choice Book. Kathy-jo currently lives with her family in the Great Lakes area.

David Geister

Creating larger-than-life characters and painting the natural beauty of the land made working on *The Legend of Wisconsin* pure fun for David Geister, who also illustrated *The Legend of Minnesota* and *The Voyageur's Paddle*, his first picture books with Sleeping Bear Press. His artwork for this story gives David a chance to share with others his love of the state where he spent his childhood.

David is well known for his story telling, and often makes appearances as historical personalities such as Revolutionary War soldier Joseph Plumb Martin and the artists Seth Eastman and George Catlin. One of David's greatest pleasures is combining his knowledge of history with his illustration work. Though he grew up in Prescott, Wisconsin, David now lives in Minneapolis with his wife, Pat Bauer, and stepdaughters, Eva and Allison.